THE ESSENTIAL HANDBOOK TO THE HIGH FIBER DIET

LOSE WEIGHT AND LOWER BLOOD SUGAR BY ADDING FIBER TO YOUR DIET INSTEAD OF COUNTING CALORIES

BY

EVELYN CARMICHAEL

Copyright © 2017

Evelyn Carmichael

The Essential Handbook to the High Fiber Diet

INTRODUCTION

Find out how fiber can help you lose weight, lower your cholesterol, and reduce your blood sugar levels without counting calories!

Losing weight is something that many people struggle with. We have been told so many times that they have to make changes to their lifestyle that they know they cannot stick to. We have been told that we are going to have to eat foods that they hate, never enjoy the foods that we love again, and spend all of their time exercising.

We have been taught wrong. Studies have proven that simply by adding more fiber to your diet, you can lose weight without restricting calories or forgoing food groups. By following the information in this book, you will learn how to make fiber a standard part of your diet.

In this book, you will learn:

- How making one small change to your diet can ensure you are able to lose weight without restricting the foods you eat or spending all of your time exercising.
- Charts depicting high fiber foods

- High Fiber recipes with pictures
- A complete chapter of high fiber desserts with pictures
- How you can ensure that you are able to eat all of the foods that you love every day while decreasing your weight and lowering your blood sugar.
- How to ensure that you are losing weight, while never counting calories, adding up points, starving, or feeling left out at parties, get-togethers, or office lunches.

The Essential Handbook to the High Fiber Diet

Evelyn Carmichael

The Essential Handbook to the High Fiber Diet

TABLE OF CONTENTS

Introduction 3
Table of Contents 7
Legal Notes 9
Forward 11
Chapter 1- How Does Fiber Impact Weight, Insulin, and Cholesterol? 15
Chapter 2- How to Increase the Fiber in Your Diet 23
Chapter 3. Fiber Charts 31
Chapter 4- High Fiber Meal Plan 37
Chapter 5- High Fiber Dessert Recipes 51
Excerpt of The Essential Handbook to Reversing Prediabetes and Diabetes 67
About The Author 73
Other Books By Evelyn Carmichael 75
    Author Note 79

Evelyn Carmichael

The Essential Handbook to the High Fiber Diet

LEGAL NOTES

Copyright © 2017 Evelyn Carmichael

All rights reserved.

All rights reserved. This book is intended for the original purchaser of this book only. No part of this book may be scanned, downloaded, reproduced, or distributed in any printed or electronic form without the written permission from the author. Please do not participate in or engage in any piracy of copyrighted materials.

Disclaimer: All content of this handbook is created for educational and informational purposes. This author is not affiliated with any specific diet plan, medical treatment, pharmaceutical or holistic company. Before any change of diet or medication, it is recommended to consult your physician. Personal use of any content is to be taken at the sole risk of the individual. The author and publisher bare no responsibility therein.

Evelyn Carmichael

The Essential Handbook to the High Fiber Diet

FORWARD

Many people today are looking for a way to lose weight and there is no shortage of advice out there. In fact, it seems that every day, there are more and more new fad diets created what claim they are the one true way to help you lose weight.

The truth is, none of these fad diets are going to help you when it comes to weight loss. Yes, they may help you to lose a bit of weight when you first start out using them, however, most of them are so restrictive that they are impossible to stick to. This means that while you may be able to lose a few pounds, you will eventually go off these diets and gain the weight back, probably even more.

Much of the time, when a person tries to lose weight using these fad diets, they eventually give up, thinking that there is no authentic way for them to lose the weight that they know they need to lose, however, there is a way for you to lose the extra pounds.

One very simple change might be all that it takes to start losing the weight, without reading all the diet books out there, without having to count calories, and without having to measure everything that goes into your body.
What is this one small change? It is simple, start eating more fiber. One recent study published in the *Annals of Internal Medicine* showed that after a year, those who ate more fiber, without changing anything else about their diet, lost only a couple of pounds less than a person following a caloric restrictive low-fat, heart-healthy diet.

It has been proven by multiple studies that people who eat a lot of fiber tend to have a healthier body weight than those that do not.

What Exactly Is Fiber?

The Essential Handbook to the High Fiber Diet

Many people know how important fiber is to their diet. They may look at the nutrition labels of the foods that they are eating and choose foods that are higher in fiber, but they do not really understand what fiber is.

Fiber is a carbohydrate that is found in whole grains, fruits, beans, and vegetables. Unlike the rest of the carbohydrates that we eat, fiber is not easy for your body to digest which means that as your body digests it, your blood sugar does not spike.

In this book, we are going to learn how fiber helps with weight loss, how you can increase the fiber in your diet, and we are even going to go over some high fiber recipes that you can use in place of your favorite foods.

You are going to learn everything, in this book, that you need to know about fiber so that you can start losing weight right away and living the healthy life that you have always dreamed of.

Evelyn Carmichael

The Essential Handbook to the High Fiber Diet

CHAPTER 1- HOW DOES FIBER IMPACT WEIGHT, INSULIN, AND CHOLESTEROL?

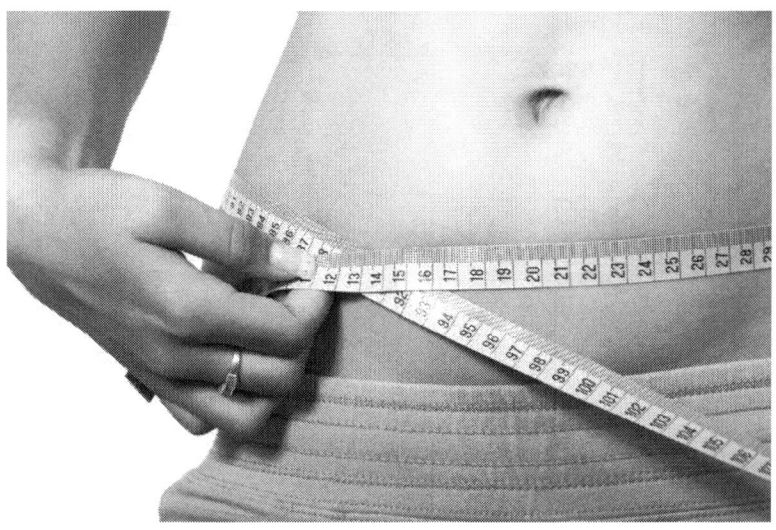

One of the reasons that many people struggle to lose weight is that it is confusing. Food is confusing, nutrition is confusing, and weight loss is confusing. Losing weight does not have to be confusing though.

Think about our ancestors, do you think that they struggled with losing weight? It is not likely that our ancestors had a tough time losing weight. We know that they were hunters and gatherers. We know that they did not have cars and most of the time, depended on their own two legs to transport them where they needed to go.

What were they doing differently? If you look at the foods that our ancestors ate, they were fruits, vegetables, grains, and meat. They did not have a cabinet full of processed foods. They ate natural foods that were packed full of fiber. According to the American Heart Association, we are supposed to make sure that we are eating plenty of fruits, vegetables, and grains each day. We should be eating fish at least twice a week- the rest of the time, eating lean protein. We are told that we need to reduce the amount of sugar that we are eating as well as our sodium and that we should reduce the amount of alcohol we drink or not drink at all.

We are also told that we need to make sure we are getting half of the calories we eat each day from carbohydrates. One fifth of our calories should come from protein, the rest should be healthy fats, except for about 7 percent of the fats should be saturated.
Just trying to understand what you are supposed to be eating sounds confusing doesn't it?

The problem with all the information that we get about what we should eat is that most of it is contradictory. The diets are so complex, they cannot be understood and few are able to succeed at using these diets.

So, instead of trying to get people to lose weight using the complicated plans of the past, researchers had decided to have participants do just one thing, increase the amount of fiber that they are eating. Calories did not need to be counted, they just needed to eat at least 30 grams of fiber per day.

When this study was done, it was found that those who were eating more fiber (30 grams per day) lost almost as much weight as those that were following a very strict weight loss regime. What this meant was that those people who participated, who were doing everything that they could to lose weight, had less than 1.5 pounds more weight loss after a full year than those who simply ate more fiber.

How can fiber help you lose weight and improve your health?

Fiber is the part of a plant that your body is not able to digest. There are two different types of fiber. The first is insoluble fiber. Insoluble fiber helps food to pass through your digestive system. The second type of fiber is soluble fiber. This type of fiber is going to help eliminate the fat from your body and it is going to help lower your cholesterol.

When you eat foods that are full of fiber, the sugars that are in the food are going to enter your bloodstream much slower than if you were to eat foods that did not contain fiber. You see, when you eat foods that do not contain fiber, your blood sugar is going to spike and then it is going to crash quickly which is going to leave you hungry. This is what causes overeating.

If you are trying to lose weight, try to eat foods that are packed with fiber. The more fiber in the food, the better it is for you. These foods also tend to be low in calories, which means that you can eat a lot of them. One of the most common complaints from people when they are on a diet is that they never feel full. However, when you eat these high fiber foods, you can eat until you are full because they have so few calories in them.

Fiber also helps you to feel fuller longer because when it reaches your stomach, it absorbs the liquid and swells. Moreover, fiber helps to reduce your blood pressure, increase blood flow, and it gives you a ton of energy, unlike sugary processed foods which usually leave you feeling more tired than before you ate.

The Essential Handbook to the High Fiber Diet

Studies have also shown that a diet high in fiber reduces LDL (or bad) cholesterol. Soluble fiber can reduce the absorption of cholesterol in your bloodstream. In fact, when you eat a food rich in soluble fiber, such as oats or beans, the fiber attaches itself to bile acids and removes them from your body. Bile acids are made by cholesterol in your liver, so when fiber takes some of these acids away, more cholesterol is "used up" to make more bile acid thereby decreasing your overall LDL cholesterol.

Another study in the *Journal of Nutrition* showed that those that ate a high fiber diet were better able to control their insulin responses and had an overall lower amount of blood glucose levels. In fact, some nutritionists working with diabetic clients recommend at least 50 grams of fiber a day to control blood sugar levels.

Most of us are not getting enough fiber. It is recommended that Americans eat at least 25 grams of fiber per day, other professionals recommend even more than that, however, the average American female is only getting 10 to 15 grams each day.

Whether you are trying to lose weight, or just trying to improve your overall health, eating more fiber is vital. How can you know if you are getting enough fiber?

Evelyn Carmichael

If you are not eating a large amount of whole grains, beans, nuts, fruits and vegetables, chances are, you are not getting enough fiber in your diet.

The Essential Handbook to the High Fiber Diet

Evelyn Carmichael

Chapter 2 - How to Increase the Fiber in Your Diet

Now that you know how important it is to your weight loss goals for you to add more fiber to your diet, you might be asking yourself how you are going to do it. The truth is, there are plenty of ways for you to get more fiber in your diet.

1. Make sure that you are getting your fiber from a wide variety of sources. Fruits, vegetables, and whole grains contain fiber. However, what many people try to do is to stick to one specific source of fiber. Instead, try to get fiber from multiple sources throughout the day. For example, oats are a great way to start the day and are going to provide you with insoluble fiber. Fruits are packed full of soluble fiber and can be added to any meal.

2. Replace the refined carbohydrates with whole grain foods. Refined carbohydrates, such as white bread have little to no fiber in them and are only going to spike your blood sugar. Instead of eating white bread, focus on eating whole grain bread such as ancient grains or 100% whole wheat which is packed with fiber. Instead of eating potato chips, eat popcorn. Instead of eating a candy bar, have an apple or a handful of nuts. Yes, you are going to have to make some changes, but they are going to be minor changes. These minor changes that you are going to make in your diet are going to lead to huge results.

3. Start the day with a fiber boost. We have all heard the saying that breakfast is the most important meal of the day. However, for some reason we think that it only means we should eat something for

breakfast, anything, even if our breakfast seems to resemble desert more than breakfast. The truth is, we love donuts, we love sugary cereal, and we love breakfast sandwiches. While these are okay to eat on occasion, they are not something that should be eaten every day. If you love cereal, try eating a bran cereal. Or try eating oats with a bit of fruit. You can also eat whole grain toast with a handful of berries on those mornings when you are in a hurry. There are plenty of options that are full of fiber and that will get your morning started out right.

4. If you are the type of person that snacks during the day, and find that you are snacking on high-fat, high calorie, sugar filled, processed junk, try replacing those snacks with high-fiber snacks. Try granola bars, trail mix, popcorn, or whole grain crackers instead. Not only are these going to give you sustainable energy, but they are going to ensure that you do not feel hungry again, minutes after you have eaten. They are going to help get you through to your next meal.

5. Include fresh fruit with every meal. Many people include fruit with their breakfast, they may even snack on fruit, but when lunch and dinner roll around, fruit is not something people think about, even though it should be. Eating fruit is a fantastic

way to get the vitamins and nutrients that you need in all of your meals. It can be used as a treat, a dessert, a snack, a side dish, and you can cook with it. The fruits that contain the highest amount of fiber are prunes, pears, oranges, berries, and apples. But don't discount some of the more exotic fruits; a mango measures in at 5 grams of fiber a serving and 1 cup of guava will boost your fiber intake by 9 grams!

6. Eat legumes by the load. This is one source of fiber that many people just don't eat. Beans, lentils, and peas are some of the best sources of fiber out there. You should try to add one serving to your meals each day. You can incorporate them into casseroles, soups, and salads, or you can make some very delicious veggie dips out of them.

7. Did you know that ethnic foods tend to be higher in fiber than American foods? One way that we ensure that we are getting enough fiber is by taking our taste buds on an adventure around the world. We regularly eat foods from around the world and do our best to try new recipes at least once a week. For example, Indian cuisine is high in legumes which boosts your fiber intake. You may find that you like one specific type of food a lot and do not like

others, but by trying ethnic cuisines, you will be increasing the fiber you are taking in.

8. Bake your own goodies and increase the fiber in them. Did you know that you can boost the amount of fiber in all of your baked goods simply by replacing the white flour with whole wheat flour? You can also add in oatmeal and fruit to your baked goods to not only make them taste even better, but to increase the fiber as well as other nutrients. This means that you don't have to say good-bye to your favorite treats while you are trying to lose weight, all you have to do is modify them a bit. Don't worry though, they are going to taste just as good as they ever did.

9. Don't try to do too much too quickly. While it is true that most people are not getting enough fiber in their diets, you do not want to make rapid changes when it comes to your diet. If you increase the amount of fiber that you are eating too quickly, it could result in a lot of gas as well as painful bloating. You need to try to increase your fiber slowly so that your gastrointestinal tract will have time to adjust to the changes. If you have specific medical issues, make sure you consult with your physician before making any dietary changes.

10. Water is very important. When you are increasing the amount of fiber that you are eating, you also need to make sure that you are increasing the amount of water that you are drinking. I stated earlier that fiber swells as it absorbs the liquid from the stomach, however, it also absorbs the water from the intestines. If you are not hydrated, the fiber can actually cause constipation. In order to avoid this, you have to make sure that you are drinking at least 64 ounces of water each day. That is only eight, 8-ounce cups of water.

11. Plan it out. Sit down with a pen and paper, think about a few slight changes that you can make in your diet, which will allow you to increase the amount of fiber that you are eating each day.

    Perhaps you can start eating oats for breakfast and replace your snacks with fruit. This would be a wonderful place to start. After a few weeks, once your body has adjusted to the increase in fiber, you could add in a few more changes, and continue to do so until you are getting the amount of fiber in your diet that your body needs.

The Essential Handbook to the High Fiber Diet

Evelyn Carmichael

Chapter 3. Fiber Charts

In the following pages, you will find charts of popular high fiber foods in the four main categories of the highest fiber foods: fruits, vegetables, legumes, and grains. For a complete listing of foods, please check out the US National Nutrient Database for Standard Reference at https://ndb.nal.usda.gov/ndb/nutrients.

Evelyn Carmichael

Fruits

	Serving Size	Fiber (g)
Raspberries	1 cup	8.0
Peaches (dried)	½ cup	6.5
Prunes	½ cup	6
Blueberries	1 cup	4.2
Pear with skin on	1 medium	6
Banana	1 medium	3.0
Apple with skin on	1 medium	3.0
Orange	1 medium	3
Grapefruit	1 medium	3
Blackberries	1/2 cup	6.5

The Essential Handbook to the High Fiber Diet

Vegetables

Vegetable	Serving	Fiber (g)
White baked potato	1 medium	5g
Spinach, cooked	½ cup	3g
Tomato	1 medium	1g
Asparagus	½ cup	2g
Broccoli (cooked)	½ cup	2g
Carrots	½ cup	2g
Cauliflower (cooked)	½ cup	2g
Baked Sweet potato	1 medium	3g

Evelyn Carmichael

Legumes

Legumes	Serving Size	Fiber (g)
Black Beans	1/2 cup	8g
Pinto Bean	1/2 cup	8g
Kidney Bean	1/2 cup	6g
Borlotti	1/2 cup	24g
Soybeans	1/2 cup	8g
Peanuts, dry-roast	1/2 cup	6g
Peas	1 cup	7g
Lentils	1/2 cup	8g
Chickpeas	1/2 cup	16g

The Essential Handbook to the High Fiber Diet

Grains

Grain	Serving	Fiber (g)
Whole Wheat Flour	1 cup	13g
Oats (cooked)	1 cup	4g
Brown Rice (cooked)	1/2 cup	2g
Quinoa (cooked)	1 cup	12g
Rye bread	1 slice	2g
White bread	1 slice	1g
Whole-wheat bread	1 slice	2g
Bran Cereal	½ cup	10g
Whole Wheat Pasta (cooked)	1 cup	4g

Evelyn Carmichael

Chapter 4 - High Fiber Meal Plan

I know how hard it can be to come up with a meal plan when you are trying to change the way that you eat or increase the fiber in your diet. Sometimes it seems as if your mind just goes completely blank.

Therefore, I am including this two-day meal plan to bring your fiber total well over 30 grams. Of course, not everyone is going to love all the foods that are listed on the meal plan, however, I hope that it will give you an idea of the types of meals that you should be eating.

Breakfast- approximately 7 grams of fiber
You will need:
1/2 of a cup of black beans (canned), drained, rinsed and heated
2 eggs, cooked, however, you like
2 tablespoons of salsa
1 tablespoon of cheddar cheese, shredded

Directions:

After you have cooked the eggs, top them with the black beans, the salsa, and the cheese.

Snack- approximately 8 grams of fiber
1 cup of raspberries

Lunch- approximately 15 grams of fiber
You will need:
1 slice of whole grain bread
2 teaspoons of Dijon mustard
3 slices of deli turkey
2 tomato slices
1 slice of cheddar cheese
1 cup of vegetable and lentil soup (recipe to follow)

Directions:
Begin by spreading the Dijon mustard on the bread and layering the turkey on. Top with the cheese and the tomato. Toast until the cheese melts. Serve with a cup of lentil soup.

Snack- approximately 6 grams of fiber
1 pear

Dinner- approximately 10 grams of fiber
2 ½ cups of Avocado Shrimp Chopped Salad (recipe found at the end of this chapter)

The Essential Handbook to the High Fiber Diet

1 baguette slice, (whole wheat) that has been drizzled with a teaspoon of avocado or olive oil as well as sprinkled with a pinch of salt.

Approximate total Fiber Day One= 46 grams

Day 2

Breakfast- approximately 13 grams of fiber
Steel Cut Oatmeal (1 Cup)
Dried Berries (1/2 cup)
Coffee (1 cup)

Snack- approximately 3 grams of fiber
1 medium banana

Lunch- approximately 12 grams of fiber
1 cup Cesar Salad
1 Bean and cheese burrito on whole wheat wrap

Snack- approximately 3 grams of fiber

Peanut butter (2 TBS) on celery

Dinner- approximately 12 grams of fiber

Salmon (8 oz) grilled

1 cup of Bean Salad (recipe to follow)

1 cup of asparagus

Approximate total Fiber for Day Two= 43 grams

Add in an extra punch of fiber by choosing a high fiber dessert from the next chapter.

The Essential Handbook to the High Fiber Diet

Bean Salad

Ingredients:

1 (14.5 ounce) can lima beans, drained
1 (14.5 ounce) can wax beans, drained
1 (15.5 ounce) can garbanzo beans, drained
1 (14.5 ounce) can kidney beans, drained
1 (14.5 ounce) can black beans, drained
1/2 cup chopped green pepper

Evelyn Carmichael

1/2 cup of red pepper
1 cup chopped onion
1/2 cup chopped tomato
1/2 cup salad oil
1/2 cup vinegar
1/2 teaspoon salt
1/2 teaspoon ground black pepper
3/4 cup white sugar

DIRECTIONS:

Combine the beans, red and green pepper, onion, and tomato in a large bowl; toss to mix.

Whisk together the oil, vinegar, salt, pepper, and sugar in a separate bowl until the sugar is dissolved; pour over the bean mixture. Refrigerate 8 hours or overnight before serving.

Note: This serves a large crowd (15-18), but lasts for several days if you keep it refrigerated. Feel free to use whatever beans you have on hand. I often add in a can of northern beans and some extra veggies like celery. Depending on what beans you use, this salad can top in at 12 grams of fiber per cup!

Avocado Shrimp Chopped Salad

Ingredients:

For the dressing:

5 tablespoons of sour cream
3 tablespoons of Extra Virgin Olive Oil (EVOO)
3 tablespoons of Apple Cider Vinegar (ACV)
2 tablespoons of freshly chopped cilantro
1 tablespoon of freshly chopped dill
1 tablespoon of minced shallot
2 garlic cloves, minced
¾ of a teaspoon of dry mustard
¼ of a teaspoon of salt

Evelyn Carmichael

For shrimp:
25 raw shrimps, deveined and peeled
2 additional tablespoons of EVOO
2 teaspoons of lime zest, finely grated
¼ of a teaspoon of salt
¼ of a teaspoon of black pepper
2 ears of corn that have been husked
4 cups of romaine lettuce, chopped
¾ of a cup of red cabbage, chopped finely
½ cup shredded carrots
¾ of a cup of red bell pepper, diced
½ of a cup of red onion, diced
½ of a cup of chopped cherry tomatoes
½ of a fennel bulb, cut in half again and then sliced thinly
1 avocado, peeled and diced

Directions:

The first thing that you are going to do is place all of the dressing ingredients in your food processor or your blender and process until they are smooth.

Next, you will want to prepare the shrimp and salad. In order to do this, you will preheat your grill to medium heat. You can also use a grill pan if needed. Place the shrimp in a bowl with 2 tablespoons of EVOO, the lime zest, salt and ¼ of a teaspoon of black pepper. Toss well.

The Essential Handbook to the High Fiber Diet

Grill your corn on the cob, turning it occasionally, and cook for about 10 minutes or until it is slightly charged. Remove the corn from the grill and place the shrimp on the grill. Cook for about 5 minutes, turning once.

Place the corn on a cutting board and cut the kernels off, then place the shrimp on the cutting board and cut into pieces that are bite-sized.

In a large bowl, place the cabbage, lettuce, onion, bell pepper, fennel, tomatoes, avocado, and bacon, then mix well. Add the corn and the shrimp as well as the dressing and toss ensuring it is all evenly coated. Season with pepper if desired.

Note: this salad works well with any vegetables/ lettuces you have on hand. If I am preparing a quick lunch and don't have time for the grill, I will use cooked shrimp instead and the recipe is just as delicious!

Evelyn Carmichael

Vegetable and Lentil Soup

Ingredients:

2 tablespoons EVOO (extra virgin olive oil)
¾ cup of onion, chopped
¾ cup of carrots (about 2), peeled and chopped
2/3 cup tomatoes (about 1 medium tomato), chopped
2/3 cup celery (about 2 stalks), chopped
1 TBS minced garlic (about 2 garlic cloves)
1 TBS sea salt
1 TBS tomato paste
1 cup of kale (chopped)
2 cups brown or green lentils

The Essential Handbook to the High Fiber Diet

1/2 tsp dried thyme
1 small bay leaf
1/4 tsp ground black pepper
6 cups chicken broth
4 cups water
2 teaspoons red wine vinegar

Directions:

In a large soup pot over high heat, add in the EVOO. Add the onion, carrots, celery, garlic, and 1 teaspoon of the salt. Reduce the heat to low and sauté until the vegetables are somewhat soft, about 5 minutes. Add the tomato and cook for 2 minutes. Stir in the tomato paste and cook for another 2 minutes.

Add the lentils, pepper, thyme, bay leaf, and the remaining 2 teaspoons salt. Add the broth and water, and bring to a boil, skimming and discarding any foam as it rises to the surface. Reduce the heat and simmer until the lentils are tender, 15 to 20 minutes. If the lentils are older, it will take longer to cook. Stir in the kale and cook for 2 more minutes. Stir in the vinegar. Season to taste with salt and pepper.

Evelyn Carmichael

Note: Add in any vegetables you wish to this tasty soup. You can also add more water at the end to get to the desired consistency.

The Essential Handbook to the High Fiber Diet

Evelyn Carmichael

Chapter 5 - High Fiber Dessert Recipes

One of the reasons that many people hate dieting is because they think that they must forgo their favorite desserts, however, there are alternative recipes that you can use to create tasty desserts while still eating a high fiber diet. As a side note, 1 oz. of dark chocolate contains 2g of fiber.

High Fiber Brownies

Ingredients:

3 cups of any all-bran cereal with extra fiber
2 ½ cups of water
1 ½ teaspoons of baking powder
2/3 cups chopped walnuts
1 box of brownie mix

The Essential Handbook to the High Fiber Diet

Directions:

Pour the 3 cups of cereal in a bowl and top with the 2 ½ cups of water. Allow this to sit for about 15 minutes. After the cereal has soaked in the water, mix in the baking powder and the boxed brownie mix. Stir well until completely blended. Do not add anything else. No other liquids are needed.

Fill your muffin cups about ½ of the way full and place the brownies in the oven. Cook at 350 degrees for about 20 minutes. This is going to make 30 medium size brownies that are not only delicious, but packed full of fiber.

Evelyn Carmichael

High Fiber Oatmeal Chocolate Chip Cookies

Ingredients:

2 sticks of butter
½ of a cup of granulated sugar
½ of a cup of brown sugar
1/3 of a cup of cocoa powder
1 teaspoon of vanilla
1 ½ cup of whole wheat flour
1 teaspoon of baking powder
3 cups of old-fashioned oats (do not use quick oats)
6 ounces of chocolate chips
½ cup raisins
2 eggs

Directions:

Place the granulated sugar, brown sugar, cocoa, vanilla, and eggs in a bowl, beat until mixed well. Then add in the flour, baking powder, oats and chocolate chips. Using your hands, mix until it becomes the consistency of cookie dough.

Place balls that are about the size of 1 tablespoon of the cookie dough on an ungreased baking sheet and bake for 7 minutes at 350 degrees.

Flax Banana Bread

Ingredients:
1 cup of whole ground flax
½ of a teaspoon of baking soda
½ of a teaspoon of baking powder
½ of a cup of walnuts, chopped
1 smashed very ripe banana
2/3 of a cup of water
2 tablespoons of EVOO
1 packet of stevia sweetener

The Essential Handbook to the High Fiber Diet

2 eggs
1 tablespoon of vanilla

Evelyn Carmichael

Directions:

Begin by grinding 1 cup of whole flax seed. Then place the ground flax seed in a bowl along with the baking soda and baking powder. Mix until completely combined.

In a second bowl, you will mix the water, eggs, oil, stevia and vanilla. Mix until completely combined. Add bananas. Add the walnuts to the first bowl which contains the dry ingredients. Grease your microwavable casserole dish (should be 8 inches in diameter).

Pour the wet ingredients into the dry ingredients and mix well. Pour the entire mixture into the casserole dish. Place in the microwave and cook on high for 5 minutes. After you take the bread out of the microwave, you will turn it upside down on your baking rack to cool.

After cooled, slice and serve. This bread is great served with berries and cream cheese.

Note: I also bake these in individual mini loafs and freeze them for a special treat. Just pour in loaves and bake at 350 for approximately 20 minutes.

Banana Bran Muffins

Ingredients:

3 cups of oat bran
3 teaspoons of baking powder
1 teaspoon of cinnamon
¼ of a teaspoon of nutmeg
1 cup of mashed bananas
½ of a cup of skim milk
2 egg whites
2 tablespoons of EVOO (extra virgin olive oil)

Evelyn Carmichael

Directions:
Begin by preheating your oven to 425 degrees. Spray your muffin cups with cooking spray or line them.

Place all the dry ingredients in one bowl and mix well. Place the banana, oil, milk and egg whites in a second bowl and mix well.

Add the wet ingredients to the dry and mix well.

Pour the mixture into your muffin tins. This recipe is going to make 6 large muffins. Bake your muffins for about 20 minutes or until they are golden brown.

Note: you can use any fruit you like to substitute the banana. I often use blueberries or raspberries or even carrot and zucchini as a substitute.

The Essential Handbook to the High Fiber Diet

Oatmeal Banana Bites

Ingredients:

1 cup of old-fashioned oats
1 banana, ripe
1 egg white
12 packets of stevia
¼ of a teaspoon of salt
½ of a teaspoon of cinnamon
¼ of a cup of apple, diced

Evelyn Carmichael

½ cup coconut flakes

Directions:

Begin by placing the banana in a bowl and mashing it. Add in the rest of the ingredients and mix well.

Roll dough into 1 inch sized balls and cover with coconut flakes. Bake the Banana Bites for about 9 minutes at 350 degrees.

Take the bites out of the oven, turn the cookie sheet around and then turn off the oven. Place them back in the warm oven for 5 more minutes.

The Essential Handbook to the High Fiber Diet

Conclusion

As you can see, increasing the fiber in your diet in order to lose weight does not mean that you have to give up all the foods that you love. The fact is that you can increase the fiber in all your favorite recipes, not just in your dessert recipes. There are so many ways for you to increase the fiber in your diet as well as in your recipes without you ever really noticing that there is no reason not to.

It is wonderful to know that you can lose weight, live a healthy lifestyle and still enjoy all the foods that you love just by increasing the amount of fiber that you eat each day.

Of course, if you want to lose weight quickly, it is always best to eat a diet filled with whole foods, get plenty of exercise, and stay hydrated, but if you simply don't have the time, or if you are looking for one small change that you can make in your diet which will make a huge difference, increasing the amount of fiber that you eat each day just might be the answer that you are looking for.

Read on for an excerpt of Evelyn Carmichael's book *The Essential Handbook to Reversing Prediabetes and Diabetes*, now on Amazon.

Evelyn Carmichael

THE ESSENTIAL HANDBOOK TO REVERSING PREDIABETES AND DIABETES

MEAL PLANS AND RECIPES TO REDUCE YOUR BLOOD SUGAR LEVELS AND ELIMINATE DIABETES AND PREDIABETES

By
EVELYN CARMICHAEL

Copyright © 2017

Evelyn Carmichael

The Essential Handbook to the High Fiber Diet

INTRODUCTION

Millions of people throughout the globe suffer from Prediabetes and Diabetes, but not everyone is aware that they can reverse it simply by changing the way they eat. If you suffer from Prediabetes or Diabetes, diet, exercise, and your overall weight can play a significant part in your blood sugar level. This book concentrates on specific foods and how you choose food that will be beneficial in reducing and even reversing your diagnosis. For those that have not been diagnosed, but have a family history of Diabetes or have seen their blood sugar levels inching up as the years go by, following this meal plan and tips could keep you from reaching a Diabetes diagnosis.

The recipes contained within this book are there to help you change your health and ultimately your life for the better. Start making yourself healthier today by using the meal plans and recipes in this book. Learn how to swap healthy ingredients to your own favorite recipes. In just a few weeks, you will be able to see changes to your blood sugar level that can reduce your need of medication or even reverse the diagnosis of Prediabetes or Diabetes all together. Plus, with your blood sugar levels stabilizing, you will feel better than you have

Evelyn Carmichael

The Essential Handbook to the High Fiber Diet

CHAPTER 1. WHAT IS DIABETES?

Millions of people around the world have been diagnosed with Prediabetes and Diabetes. In fact, approximately 12% of Americans over 20 years of age have been diagnosed with Diabetes. This disorder occurs when the food you eat is not properly processed as energy. Most of the food we eat is turned into glucose, or sugar, which our body uses for energy. The pancreas, an organ that lies near the stomach, makes a hormone called insulin to help glucose get into the cells of our bodies. When you have Diabetes, your body either doesn't make enough insulin or can't use its own insulin as well as it should. This causes sugars to build up in your blood.
Diabetes can cause serious health complications including heart disease, nerve damage, kidney failure, strokes, dental disease, eye problems, and lower-extremity amputations. Diabetes is the seventh leading cause of death in the United States.

According to the Center for Disease Control and Prevention, these are some of the symptoms of Diabetes: Frequent urination, excessive thirst, unexplained weight loss, extreme hunger, sudden vision changes, tingling or numbness in hands or feet, feeling very tired much of the time, very dry skin, sores that are slow to heal, and more infections than usual.

Evelyn Carmichael

There are three main types of Diabetes:

TYPE 1 DIABETES

If you have type 1 Diabetes, your body does not make insulin and in fact destroys the cells in your pancreas that makes the insulin. Type 1 Diabetes is usually diagnosed in children and young adults, although it can appear at any age. People with type 1 Diabetes need to take insulin every day to stay alive.

GESTATIONAL DIABETES

Gestational Diabetes develops in some women when they are pregnant. It is estimated to effect 2-5% of all pregnancies. Most of the time, this type of Diabetes goes away after the baby is born. However, if you've had Gestational Diabetes, you have a greater chance of developing type 2 Diabetes later in life.

TYPE 2 DIABETES

If you have Type 2 Diabetes, your body does not make or use insulin well. You can develop type 2 Diabetes at any age, even during childhood. However, this type of Diabetes occurs most often in middle-aged and older people. There is a correlation between being overweight and a genetic history with Type 2 Diabetes. Type 2 is the most common type of Diabetes with over 95% of all Diabetes diagnosis being in this category.

The Essential Handbook to the High Fiber Diet

Prediabetes

Prediabetes, also known as Borderline Diabetic, is a growing disorder. Prediabetes means that your blood sugar level is higher than normal but not yet high enough to be Type 2 Diabetes. Without lifestyle changes, people with Prediabetes are very likely to progress to Type 2 Diabetes. According to the Centers for Disease Control and Prevention, more than 86 million Americans have Prediabetes which is 1 out of 3 Americans. To make matters worse, 9 out of 10 people do not even know they have it.

This book will focus on Type 2 Diabetes and Prediabetes and the ability that food has to reverse or considerably change the severity of these conditions. If you have been diagnosed with Prediabetes or Diabetes, please make sure you discuss with your doctor any planned changes to your diet.

To find out more about Reversing Diabetes please visit here.

Evelyn Carmichael

ABOUT THE AUTHOR

Evelyn Carmichael

Evelyn was in the world of corporate finance before switching her life path after a successful battle with breast cancer. She is a personal life coach, fitness guru, and healthy lifestyle advocate.

Find out more on [Facebook](#) or at https://www.amazon.com/Evelyn-Carmichael/e/B01MQYHZLC

Evelyn Carmichael

The Essential Handbook to the High Fiber Diet

OTHER BOOKS BY EVELYN CARMICHAEL

Evelyn is the author of the Essential Handbook Series.

Her titles include the following:

The Essential Handbook to Lectin

The Essential Handbook to the Alzheimer's Diet

The Essential Handbook to Superfood Smoothies

The Essential Handbook to Hashimoto's

The Essential Handbook to Herbal Remedies

The Essential Handbook to Hygge

Evelyn Carmichael

The Essential Handbook to Diabetic Instant Pot Cooking

The Essential Handbook to Gluten Free Instant Pot Cooking

The Essential Handbook to Avocados The Superfood that Reduce Inflammation and lowers blood sugar, blood pressure, and your cholesterol

The Essential Handbook to Reversing Prediabetes and Diabetes: Meal Plans and Recipes to Reduce Your Blood Sugar Levels and Eliminate Diabetes and Prediabetes

The Essential Handbook to Turmeric and Ginger: The Anti-Inflammatory Duo that will Change your Life

The Essential Handbook to the High Fiber Diet

<u>The Essential Handbook to Coconut Oil: Tips, Recipes, and How to use for weight loss and in your daily life</u>

<u>The Essential Handbook to Apple Cider Vinegar: Tips and Recipes for Weight Loss and Improving your Health, Beauty, & Home</u>

<u>The Art of Keeping Goals</u>

<u>The Essential Handbook for Choosing the Right Diet: A Guide to the Most Popular Diets and if They are Right for You</u>

<u>The Essential Handbook to Natural Living</u>

<u>The Essential Handbook to Essential Oils: Tips and Recipes for Weight Loss, Stress Relief, and Pain Management</u>

Knee Supports: Uses, Exercises, and Benefits

Evelyn Carmichael

AUTHOR NOTE

If you enjoyed this book, found it useful or otherwise then I'd really appreciate it if you would post a short review on Amazon. I do read all the reviews personally so that I can continually write what people are wanting.

Thanks for your support!

Evelyn Carmichael